World
Fascinating Facts For Kids

David Railton

All rights reserved. No part of this publication may be reproduced in any form or by any means, including scanning, photocopying, or otherwise without prior written permission of the copyright holder. Copyright David Railton © 2019

This book is just one of a series of "Fascinating Facts For Kids" books. For more fascinating facts about people, history, animals and much more please visit:

www.fascinatingfactsforkids.com

Contents

Introduction... 1

The Outbreak of War............................... 2

First Battles... 6

The Eastern Front................................... 8

Britain in the War................................... 10

The World at War.................................... 13

Gallipoli.. 15

The Western Front.................................. 18

Verdun.. 20

The Battle of the Somme........................ 23

Revolution in Russia............................... 25

The USA Enters the War........................ 28

The War at Sea.. 31

The War in the Air.................................. 34

The Spring Offensives............................ 37

Armistice & Peace Conference.............. 39

Conclusion.. 41

Illustration Attributions........................ 42

Introduction

In the early 20th century, there was a lot of tension between the countries of Europe. This hostility and distrust was to lead to a war which was to be fought throughout the world, claiming millions of lives.

Over the years, the powerful European countries had formed alliances and partnerships with each other and by 1914 they had settled into two groups. On the one side were Germany, the Austrian-Hungarian Empire and Italy, and on the other were Britain, France and Russia.

These great powers were building massive armies and navies, which regularly fought each other across the world as they tried to build or defend their overseas empires. The technology of the day meant that the weapons made were more powerful and destructive than anything seen before.

Europe was like a barrel of dynamite waiting to explode and it would need just one spark to start a war unlike any other in history. That spark came on June 28 1914.

I hope the following facts will fascinate you and encourage you to find out more about a terrible war which changed the world.

The Outbreak of War

1. In 1914 the Austrian-Hungarian Empire controlled much of south-east Europe, including the region of Bosnia. The people of Bosnia wanted the Austrian-Hungarians to leave their country so that they could join Serbia, a neighboring country with which they had much in common.

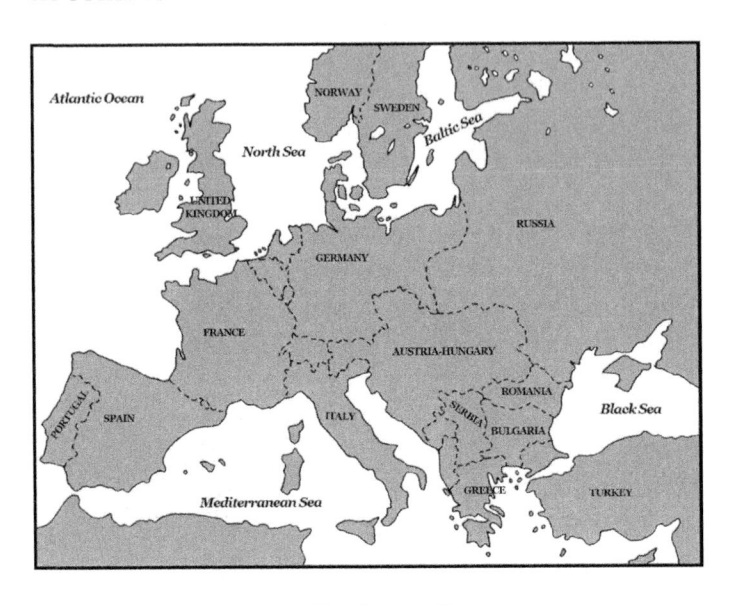

Europe before the war

2. Many Bosnians formed terrorist groups to fight the Austrian-Hungarians and get them out of their country. One of these groups, called the "Black Hand", decided to assassinate the nephew of the Austrian-Hungarian Emperor, who was to visit the Bosnian city of Sarajevo.

3. Archduke Franz Ferdinand and his wife, Countess Sofia, were being driven through Sarajevo on June 28, when the Black Hand group carried out its attack. The first two attempts failed, but later that morning 19-year-old Gavrilo Princip got close enough to the car to shoot and kill the Archduke and his wife.

Gavrilo Princip

4. The Austrian-Hungarians were outraged and decided to punish Serbia for the assassination of the Archduke. The Serbians were given a list of demands to agree to and although they agreed to eight of them, the Austrian-Hungarians were not satisfied and on July 28, they declared war on Serbia.

5. Russia, an ally of Serbia, offered to help and began to prepare its Army for war. Germany, a powerful ally of the Austrian-Hungarians, declared war on Russia and its other ally, France.

6. Germany was now at war on both its eastern and western borders, against Russia and France, but they had been preparing for years for such a situation.

7. The Germans knew that it would take weeks for Russia to get its Army ready for war and during this time they could defeat France, after which they could deal with the Russians.

8. The French had built strong defensive fortifications along its border with Germany. In order to invade France, Germany avoided these fortifications by ruthlessly marching through Belgium and Luxembourg, before turning towards the French capital, Paris.

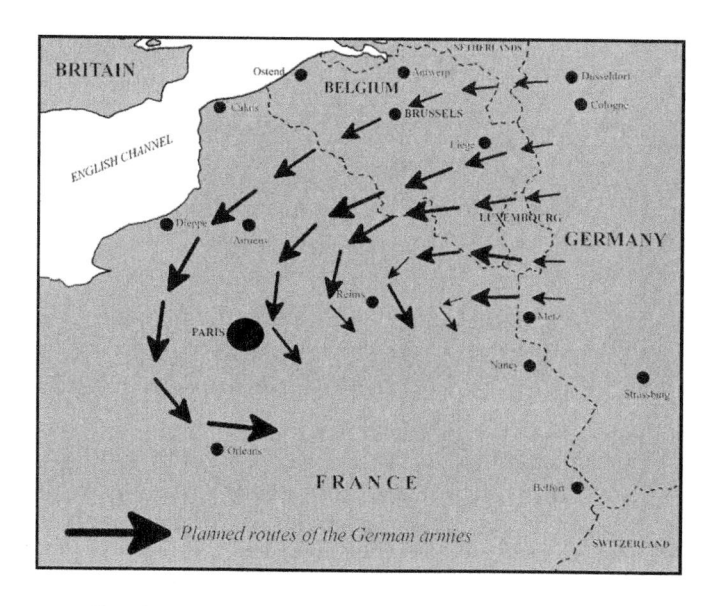

The invasion of France by Germany

9. The British had an agreement to protect Belgium and when the Germans invaded the country on August 4, Britain was brought into the war against Germany. It had taken just eight days from the assassination in Sarajevo for Europe to be plunged into conflict.

First Battles

10. The first battle of the war began on August 23 near the city of Mons, on the France/Belgium border. The Germans overpowered the French and British armies and continued towards Paris.

11. By September, the Germans had reached the River Marne, just 30 miles from the French capital, but its soldiers were exhausted by their long march from Germany. The British and French armies arrived and forced the enemy back for 40 miles, where the Germans began digging trenches from which they could defend themselves.

12. The French and British were unable to dislodge the Germans from their defensive positions and so they started to dig trenches of their own. Before long, the trenches stretched for 400 miles from the English Channel to Switzerland, forming the "Western Front".

Western Front 1914

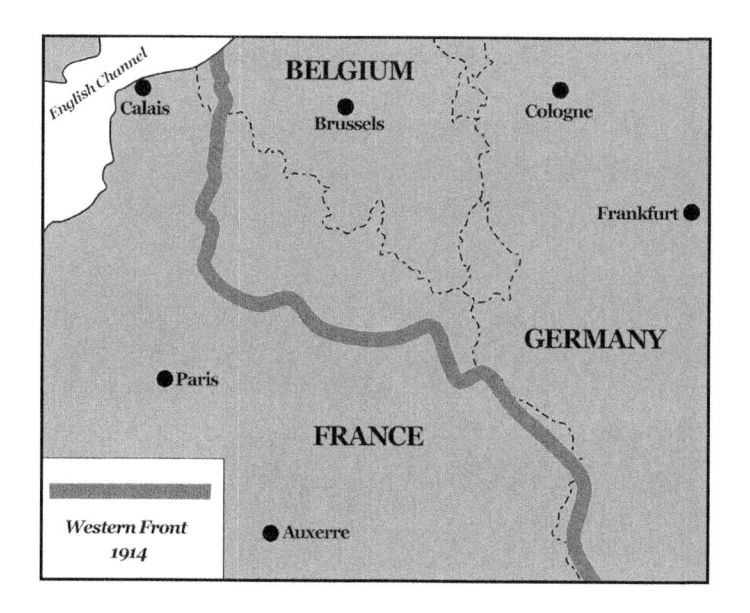

13. When the war began it was thought that it would be over by Christmas, but the trenches meant that it was difficult for either side to move anywhere. It now looked as though the war was going to be a long one.

The Eastern Front

14. On August 17 Russia invaded a part of Germany called East Prussia, which meant that Germany was fighting in both the west and the east.

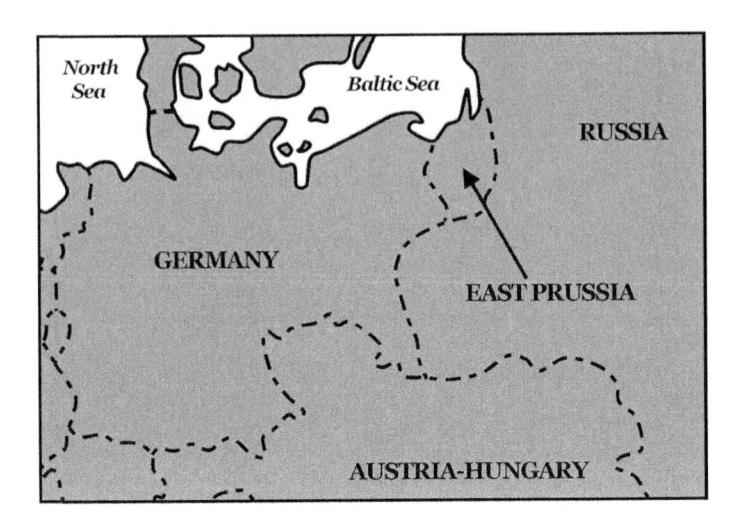

15. Even though the German Army was split between the Western and Eastern Fronts, it inflicted a heavy defeat on the Russian Army at the Battle of Tannenberg.

16. The Battle of Tannenberg was Russia's heaviest defeat of the war and was followed a few days later by another defeat at the Battle of the Masurian Lakes.

17. Germany's ally, Austria-Hungary, was also fighting in the east against both Russia and Serbia. She was not doing very well though and had to be regularly helped out by the Germans, which stretched the German Army even further.

18. The war in the east was totally different to the slow-moving trench warfare in the west, as both sides advanced and retreated constantly, gaining and losing territory all the time.

Britain in the War

19. All countries during World War I were using massive armies and more and more men were needed to fight. By the end of 1915 over two million men had volunteered to join the British Army.

An Army recruitment poster

20. The new and more powerful weapons of the time were killing and injuring large numbers of men. These soldiers needed replacing urgently and in January 1916, volunteering was stopped when the British government introduced conscription. This forced men to join the armed forces to fight for their country.

21. It was not just men who were affected by the war. Women, who had not been expected to go out to work before, had to take over the jobs of the men who went to war.

Women at work in a factory

22. Unlike in earlier wars, when only the armies and navies were involved, World War I also saw the ordinary people of Britain affected. Germany launched air raids from air ships called "Zeppelins", which killed 557 British civilians over the duration of the war. The German Navy also fired shells at the British coast.

A German Zeppelin

23. There was outrage in Britain in May 1915, when a German submarine attacked and sank the "Lusitania", a British cruise liner sailing off the coast of Ireland. Over 1,000 civilians lost their lives, but the Germans thought that the attack was justified as the "Lusitania" had been carrying ammunition as well as people.

The World at War

24. Many countries of Europe had built empires, controlling countries in other parts of the world. The British Empire was by far the largest and many of its colonies joined the war to fight on Britain's side.

25. The British colonies included Australia, New Zealand, Canada, South Africa and India. These countries sent their men either to fight in Europe or to capture German colonies in their parts of the world.

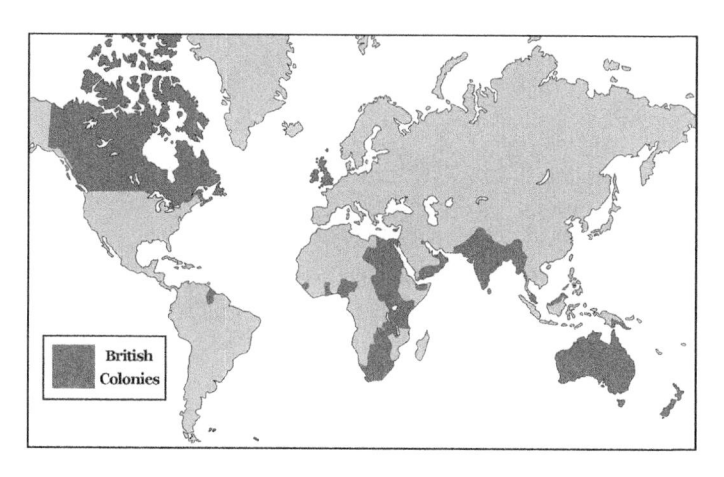

26. In the Far East, Japan wanted to be thought of as a powerful and important country and decided to join the war on the side of Britain and its allies. She captured all the German controlled islands in the northern Pacific Ocean, as well as a German naval base at Tsingtao in north-east China.

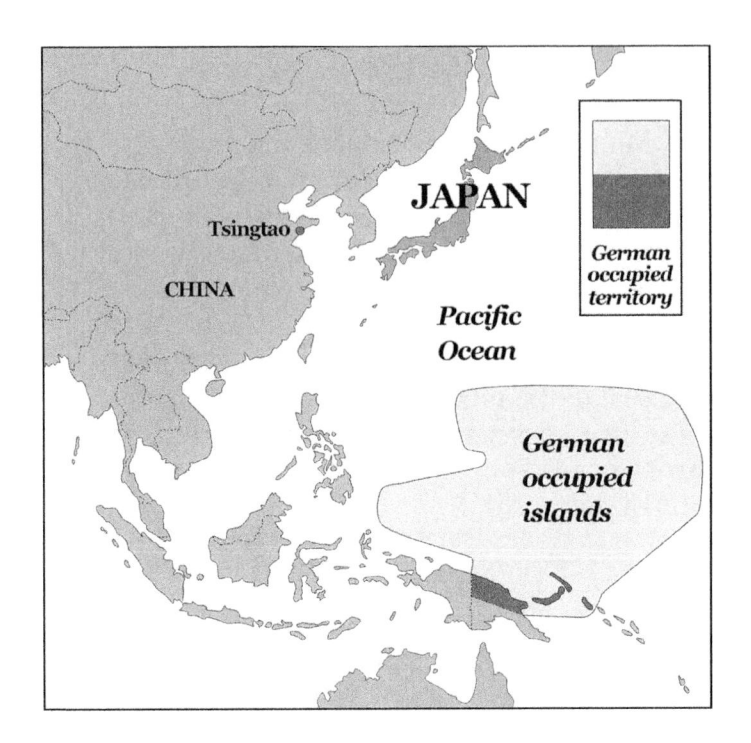

27. Although the war had started off as a European war, by 1916 virtually every part of the world had become affected by it, making it the first ever world war in history.

Gallipoli

28. In October 1914 Turkey entered the war on the side of Germany and began attacking the Russians. The ruler of Russia, Tsar Nicholas II, asked Britain and her allies for help.

29. Winston Churchill, the First Lord of the Admiralty, who was in charge of the British Royal Navy, sent a fleet of battleships to the Dardanelles, a narrow stretch of water which separates mainland Turkey from the peninsular of Gallipoli.

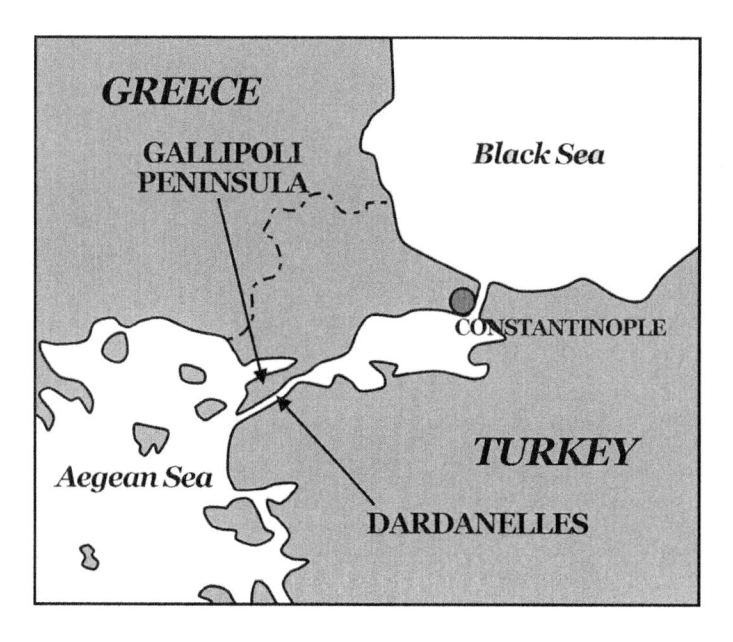

30. The British and French ships planned to destroy the Turkish defenses so that the allied navies could sail up the Dardanelles to capture the Turkish capital, Constantinople. Instead, the Turks sank half of the allied fleet. It was decided that soldiers would be needed as well as the Navy.

31. A force of mainly Australian and New Zealand soldiers was sent to the Gallipoli peninsula in April 1915. They had been supplied with out-of-date maps and landed in the wrong place. They were attacked by the Turks and suffered dreadful casualties.

Australian troops at Gallipoli

32. The Allies launched another attack in August, but again the Turks were ready for them. The allied soldiers were pinned down by the Turks for months until an evacuation was ordered.

33. The Gallipoli campaign was a disaster for the Allies, particularly Australia and New Zealand, and was seen by many as a pointless loss of life. The Allies lost around 200,000 lives and the Turks lost at least that number.

The Western Front

34. By 1916 both sides had established their systems of trenches. Life for the soldiers was tedious, filthy and cold, with occasional moments of terror.

Life in a trench

35. The Allies' plan to gain an advantage was to fire shells at the German trenches to flatten their defensive barbed wire, and then send soldiers across the short distance between the German and allied trenches. On reaching the enemy, they would attack with rifles and bayonets.

36. The shells falling on the German trenches caused only limited damage and the Germans protected themselves in strong underground

bunkers. When the allied soldiers approac
the Germans were able to shoot large numbe
them easily with their machine guns.

37. The Western Front settled into years of deadlock and stalemate, waiting for breakthroughs which rarely came.

38. Many soldiers were affected by "shellshock", the constant stress shattering their nerves. 80,000 British soldiers suffered from shellshock over the duration of the war.

39. Many soldiers who were unable to cope simply ran away, deserting their posts. The punishment for this was severe, with over 900 allied soldiers being executed for desertion or cowardice.

40. A new method of killing was introduced during the Second Battle of Ypres in April 1915. The Germans released poisonous chlorine gas from nearly 6,000 cylinders, which floated over to the French trenches, causing panic and many casualties.

41. The use of gas became commonplace for the rest of the war and was used by both sides. Many different types of gas were used and could cause painful and lingering deaths. Those that survived suffered from the effects of the gas for the rest of their lives.

Verdun

42. By the end of 1915 Germany had decided that Britain, not France, was the main enemy, but to get to Britain they first had to defeat the French Army.

43. The German plan was to launch an attack that would bring every available French soldier to fight them. Germany could then destroy the French Army and concentrate on defeating Britain.

44. On February 21 1916 the Germans lined up 1,400 guns and began bombarding Verdun, an ancient town that was steeped in French history. 190,000 French soldiers were sent there to defend the town to the last.

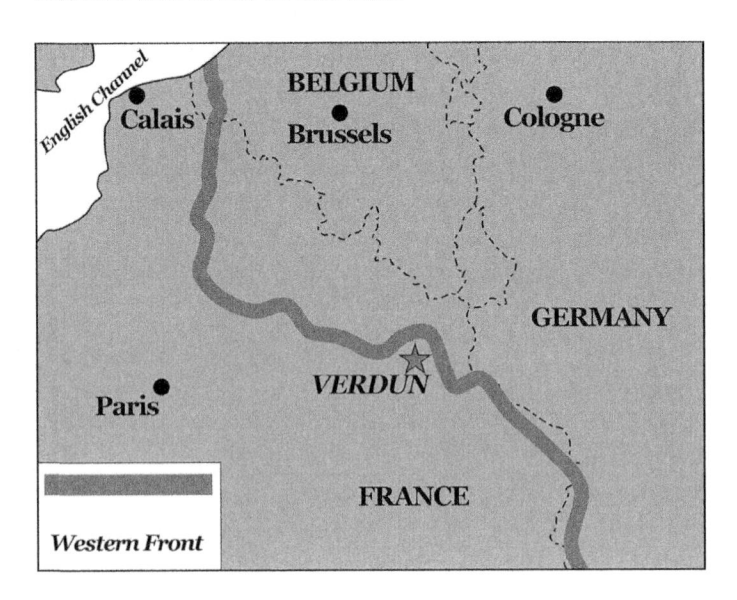

Western Front

45. The French defended Verdun vigorously. They managed to keep the only road into the town open, which meant they could bring in supplies and more soldiers. Every day, around 2,000 trucks made the dangerous journey along the road into Verdun.

46. The battle raged for months with neither side gaining a significant advantage, but that situation was to change.

German prisoners at Verdun

47. In June, over on the Eastern front, the Austrian-Hungarians were being attacked by the Russians and appealed for Germany's help once again. Germany sent men from Verdun to Austria-Hungary's aid, and around the same time, the British started the Battle of the Somme in an attempt to relieve the pressure at Verdun.

The French were now able to hold on to Verdun in the longest battle of the war.

48. Verdun was a terrible battle in which at least 500,000 men lost their lives. It was though, a magnificent and heroic victory for the French, with its Army coming close to destruction.

The Battle of the Somme

49. The Battle of the Somme was meant to be a decisive breakthrough for the Allies but it turned out to be a waste of one million lives for the gain of just five miles (eight km). The battle was fought mainly by inexperienced British volunteers as the French were occupied in trying to hold onto Verdun.

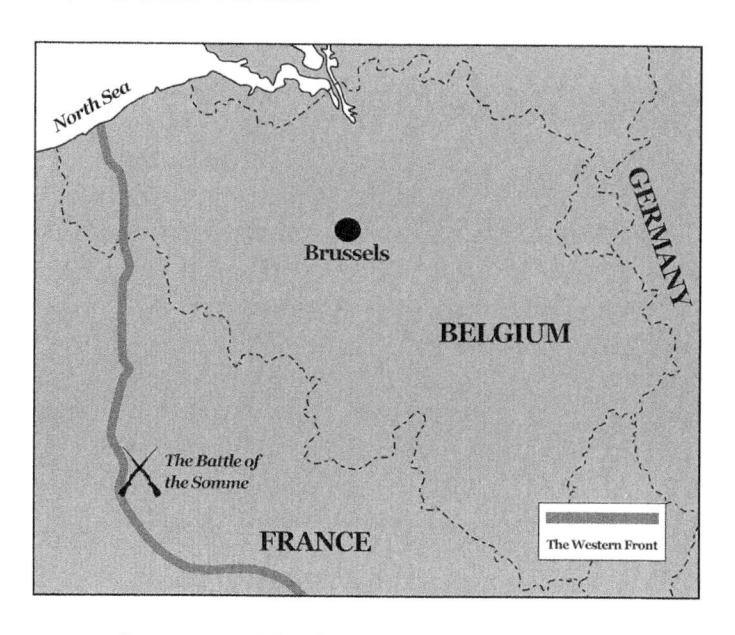

50. The start of the battle saw five days of shelling from the British to flatten the barbed wire which was defending the German trenches. When the shelling was finished the plan was for the British to cross the "No Man's Land" separating the two sets of trenches, to take on any Germans who had survived.

Soldiers crossing "No Man's Land"

51. When the shelling stopped on July 1, line after line of British soldiers was ordered across to the German trenches. The barbed wire had suffered little damage and many Germans had survived, able to gun down the helpless British soldiers with ease.

52. The first day of the Battle of the Somme was the worst day that the British Army had ever suffered. There were over 57,000 casualties on that one day alone, including over 19,000 dead.

53. The battle continued for four-and-a-half months, finally ending on November 18. The British lost about 400,000 men, the French 200,000 and the Germans 400,000. The hoped for breakthrough had not happened and neither side had gained any great advantage.

Revolution in Russia

54. Russia was ruled by Tsar Nicholas II and his family, the Romanovs. Following a series of defeats of the Russian Army, the Tsar put himself in charge, even though he had no military experience.

Tsar Nicholas II

55. The Russian people were not happy with being ruled by the Tsar, the way the war was going or the severe shortage of food. They made their feelings known on March 8 1917, when they staged a demonstration in the Russian capital, Petrograd.

56. The demonstration quickly turned into a revolution and two million soldiers who had been loyal to the Tsar deserted the Army and went home.

57. The Russian people forced the Tsar to step down, ending 300 years of rule by the Romanovs. A new government was formed, led by Alexander Kerensky, who was determined to carry on fighting the war.

58. Most Russians wanted an end to the war, including Vladimir Lenin, who was leader of the Bolshevik political party. The Bolsheviks were committed to giving ordinary people more power.

Vladimir Lenin

59. Lenin had not been in Russia at the time of the Revolution, but when he arrived in Petrograd he made speeches attacking Kerensky and the war, and called for an overthrow of the government.

60. Kerensky gave orders to arrest all Bolsheviks and Lenin fled to Finland, a neighboring country of Russia.

61. Lenin secretly returned to Russia in October 1917 and the Bolsheviks seized control of government buildings, arrested members of the government and declared Lenin the leader of Russia.

62. On December 16 Russia made peace with Germany, but was forced to give much of her territory to the Germans. Now, Germany had only one front to fight a war on.

The USA Enters the War

63. At the beginning of the last century, like today, the most powerful country in the world was the United States of America. Britain and France repeatedly tried to persuade the Americans to join the war, but American policy was to remain neutral and not get involved.

64. When the "Lusitania" was sunk by German submarines in May 1915, 128 Americans were among those who drowned. There was outrage in America and the incident paved the way for the United States to enter the war.

The "Lusitania"

65. During 1916, although most Americans were in favor of staying out of the war, a growing number thought that they should help the Allies defeat Germany.

66. The "Lusitania" was not the only non-naval ship that the Germans sunk. Americans were also enraged that German submarines were sinking great numbers of merchant ships without giving a warning, which was breaking one of the accepted rules of war.

67. Although Woodrow Wilson, the American president, thought that war was evil, he thought that the Allies were on the side of right and that the Germans were in the wrong.

Woodrow Wilson

68. The final incident which brought the United States into the war came in January 1917. The Germans planned to get Mexico to declare war on the United States and Germany would make sure that Mexico got back territory that the Americans had taken from them the previous century.

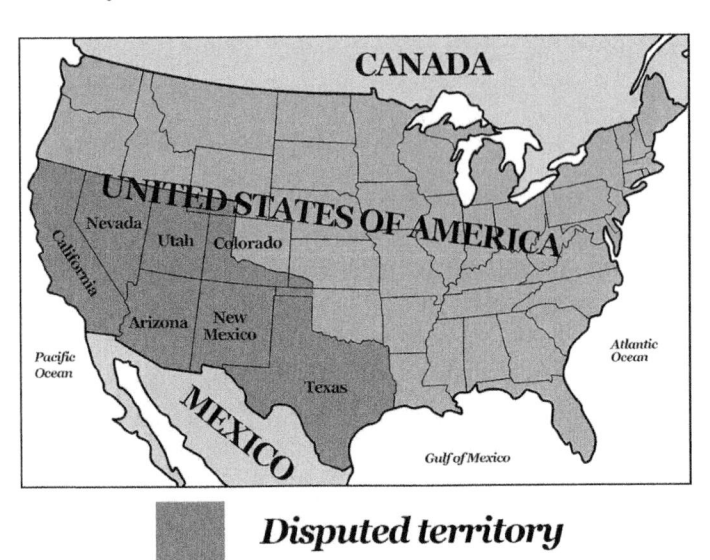

Disputed territory

69. The British found out about this plan and told the Americans. Again there was outrage and on April 6 1917, the United States declared war on Germany. The first American soldiers arrived in Europe in June and were to play a major part in the defeat of Germany the following year.

The War at Sea

70. Britain, being an island, depended on ships to bring food and supplies across the Atlantic Ocean from the United States and Canada. If Germany could stop the ships from North America reaching their destinations, then Britain would starve.

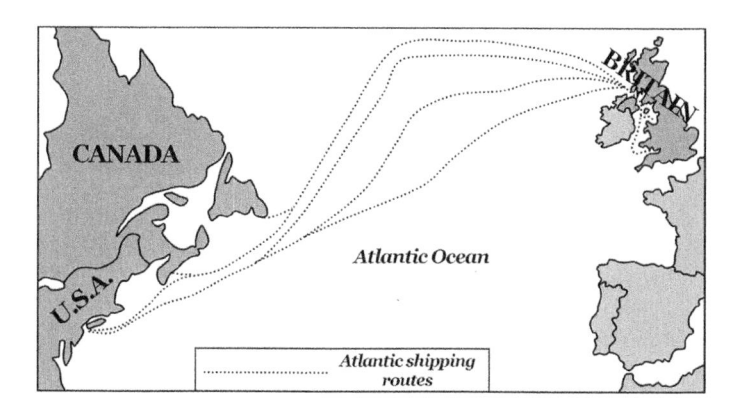

71. The British Navy was very powerful and had more ships than the German Navy, so the Germans decided to use submarines to attack ships crossing the Atlantic.

72. The German submarines, called U-Boats, had great early success, sinking a quarter of all the ships trying to reach Britain.

73. The British solved the problem by using a convoy system, where the ships traveled together in large groups protected by the Navy, rather than travelling alone.

An Atlantic convoy in 1943

74. The only time the British and German navies fought each other was in May 1916 at the Battle of Jutland, which took place off the coast of Denmark. There was no clear victor and the Germans decided to concentrate on its use of submarines.

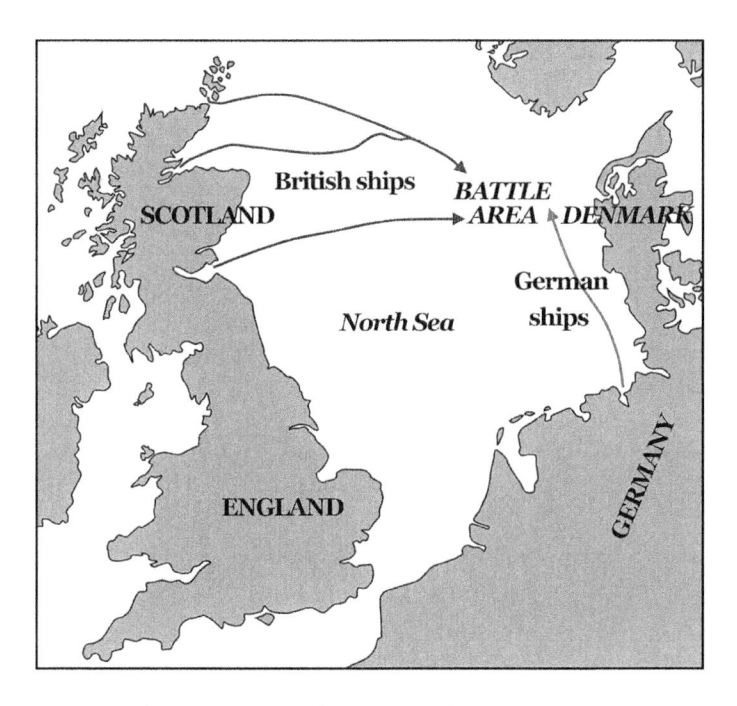

The Battle of Jutland, May 1916

The War in the Air

75. The first powered flight had taken place just 11 years before the start of World War I, so the idea of using airplanes in war was new.

76. Early airplanes were slow and at the start of the war were just used for observation. As the war progressed, they became faster and more powerful and were used to attack the enemy.

World War I airplanes

77. At first, the pilots carried rifles or revolvers to fire at the enemy, before machine guns were attached to the wings.

78. In 1915 a way was found to fire machine guns through the propeller. Now, the gun could be placed directly in front of the pilot so that he could aim more accurately.

79. The airplanes of both sides became involved in fights in the air against each other, known as "dog fights", and the pilots became famous for their acts of bravery.

80. The most famous of the pilots, or "aces" as they were known, was a German called Manfred von Richthofen, nicknamed the "Red Baron". He brought down 80 allied planes before being shot down himself in April 1918.

The "Red Baron"

81. Both airplanes and airships were used as bombers in World War I, causing major damage to cities such as Paris, London and Cologne.

82. In Britain, the Royal Flying Corps was a part of the Army and Navy, but on April 1 1918 it became independent when the Royal Air Force was formed.

The Spring Offensives

83. In 1918, with the Russians no longer at war, German soldiers who had been fighting in the east were sent to the Western Front. Germany now looked in a strong position, but they needed to crush the allied armies before the Americans arrived in numbers.

84. On March 21 1918 Germany launched the first of their "Spring Offensives" to try to finally defeat Britain, France and their allies. One million shells were fired in just five hours and the Germans were able to advance 50 miles, devastating the allied armies.

British soldiers relaxing during the Spring Offensives

85. Despite its success, the German Army lost over 200,000 men and was exhausted. By now, the Americans were arriving - by May there were 650,000 American soldiers in France with tens of thousands more arriving every week.

86. The arrival of the American Army lifted the spirits of the Allies and although the Americans were inexperienced in battle, they were fresh and keen to fight. During one battle, the French advised the Americans to retreat but received the reply, "Retreat? Hell, we just got here".

87. Things were now looking serious for the Germans as the Allies won back the ground that had been lost. By September, Germany's allies - Austria-Hungary, Bulgaria and Turkey had all surrendered and Germany was now fighting alone.

88. Germany was now staring defeat in the face - soldiers were deserting the Army and in the Navy the sailors were refusing to fight. Back in Germany there was unrest among the population, and the country's leaders feared there would be a revolution. Germany's leaders decided to approach the Allies to talk about putting an end to the war.

Armistice & Peace Conference

89. Representatives of the Germans and the Allies met on November 9th and the Germans were given a list of demands to end the war. They had no choice to agree to these demands and an armistice was signed, bringing peace at 11 o'clock in the morning two days later - "the eleventh hour of the eleventh day of the eleventh month".

90. Two months later, politicians from 32 countries met in Paris to settle on the punishment for Germany and her allies. The Austrian-Hungarian Empire ceased to exist and the map of Europe was re-drawn, but it was Germany's punishment that was to be particularly harsh.

91. Germany was to lose vast areas of her territory, including all her overseas colonies. Her Army was to be cut to 100,000 men, the Navy to just 15,000 and she was not allowed to have an air force. She would also have to hand over the equivalent in today's money of $440 billion to pay for damage inflicted during the war. They also had to admit that the war was their fault.

92. There was great resentment throughout Germany at the scale of their punishment and the humiliation they were suffering. These feelings were to play some part in the rise over the next 20 years of Adolf Hitler and the Nazis.

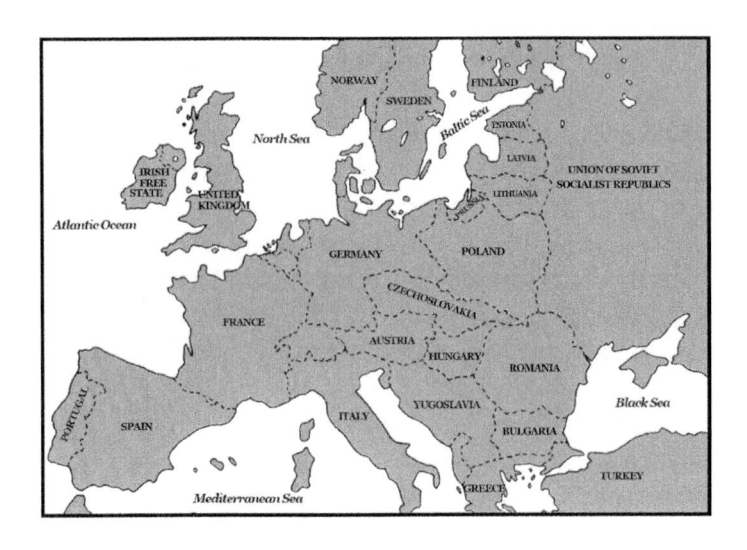

Europe after the war

Conclusion

The guns were now silent across Europe and the rest of the world, as the damage caused by the war began to be repaired.

It is estimated that at least 10 million soldiers lost their lives during the four years of the war and that 20 million were wounded. Millions of civilians also died from disease and starvation.

World War I could have been avoided had the politicians made different decisions, but tragically not only were millions killed and wounded, but the foundations were laid for an even worse world war just 20 years later.

For more fascinating facts about people, history, animals and more please visit:

www.fascinatingfactsforkids.com

Illustration Attributions

Title page
Ernest Brooks [Public domain]

Gavrilo Princip
{{PD-US}}

An Army recruitment poster
Alfred Leete

Women at work in a factory
Nicholls Horace

Australian troops at Gallipoli
www.goodfreephotos.com

Life in a trench
Btb.jo

Soldiers crossing "No Man's Land"
Geoffrey Malins

Tsar Nicholas II
A. A. Pasetti [Public domain]
{{PD-US}}

Vladimir Lenin
Wilhelm Plier [Public domain]
{{PD-US}}

The Battle of Jutland, May 1916
Grandiose [CC BY-SA 3.0 (https://creativecommons.org/licenses/by-sa/3.0)]

World War I airplanes
11Amanda [CC BY-SA 4.0 (https://creativecommons.org/licenses/by-sa/4.0)]

The "Red Baron"
{{PD-US}}
C. J. von Dühren [Public domain]

British soldiers at the Spring Offensives
John Warwick Brooke [Public domain]

Printed in Great Britain
by Amazon